Our Great Prime Ministers

By Helaine Becker and Michael Szasz

Managing Editor Barbara Campbell
Deputy Managing Editor Vineetha Mokkil
Project Editor Arpita Nath
Assistant Editor Kritika Gupta
Managing Art Editor Neha Ahuja Chowdhry
Art Editor Rashika Kachroo
Jacket Editor Francesca Young
Jacket Designers Dheeraj Arora, Amy Keast
Senior Cartographer Mohammad Hassan
DTP Designers Ashok Kumar, Vijay Kandwal, Dheeraj Singh
Picture Researcher Sakshi Saluja
Senior Producer, Pre-Production Nikoleta Parasaki
Producer Niamh Tierney
Art Director Martin Wilson
Publisher Sarah Larter

First Edition, 2017
DK Canada
320 Front Street West, Suite 1400
Toronto, Ontario M5V 3B6

Library and Archives Canada Cataloguing in Publication
Becker, Helaine, 1961–, author
Our great prime ministers: Canada's government in action / Helaine Becker and Michael Szasz.
Includes index.

ISBN: 978-1-55363-285-6 (softcover)
1. Prime ministers--Canada--Biography--Juvenile literature.
2. Canada--Politics and government--Juvenile literature.
I. Szasz, Michael, author II. Title.
FC26.P7B42 2017   j971.009'9   C2016-907455-2

DK books are available at special discounts when purchased in bulk for corporate sales, sales promotions, premiums, fund-raising, or educational use. For details, please contact specialmarkets@dk.com.

Printed and bound in China.

The publisher would like to thank the following for their kind permission to reproduce their photographs:
(Key: a-above; b-below/bottom; c-centre; f-far; l-left; r-right; t-top)
1 123RF.com: Denis Roger. **4 Alamy Stock Photo**: Pacific Press (cra). **6 iStockphoto.com**: GatorDawg (t). **8 123RF.com**: Georgios Kollidas (tl). **11 Library and Archives Canada**: (cla, ca, cra). **12 123RF.com**: Michel Loiselle (bl). **14 Library and Archives Canada**: (clb). **16 123RF.com**: Marcbruxelle (t). **17 123RF.com**: Leonard Zhukovsky (b). **18 123RF.com**: Alexandr Kovalenko (b). **21 Reuters**: Jason Franson / Pool (t). **23 Alamy Stock Photo**: Reuters / Mike Cassese (cb). **24 Alamy Stock Photo**: JSMimages (t). **26 Getty Images**: Chris Roussakis / AFP (t). **27 Getty Images**: Donald Weber (b). **28 Library and Archives Canada**: William James Topley (bl). **30 The Canadian Press**: John Woods (cl). **32 The Canadian Press**: Ron Polling (bl). **33 Alamy Stock Photo**: Reuters (tl). **34 Reuters**: Jim Young JY / GN (cla). **37 Alamy Stock Photo**: Reuters / Andy Clark (cla). Reuters: Jonathan Hayward / Pool (br). **38 The Canadian Press**: Peter Bregg (cb). **40 Alamy Stock Photo**: Reuters / Chris Wattie (t). **42 Alamy Stock Photo**: Chris Roussakis / Xinhua (ca). **43 Alamy Stock Photo**: Reuters / Chris Wattie (t). **46 Reuters**: Chris Wattie (t). **47 Alamy Stock Photo**: Reuters / Chris Wattie (b). **48 Alamy Stock Photo**: Reuters / Todd Korol (cr). **50 Alamy Stock Photo**: Reuters / Chris Wattie (cl). **51 Alamy Stock Photo**: Reuters / Chris Wattie (b). **56 Alamy Stock Photo**: Reuters (b). **58 Alamy Stock Photo**: Historic Collection (br); Tim Graham (cla/Brian Mulroney); Sputnik (ca/Jean Chretien); Victor Biro (ca/Stephen Harper); LJ Mil (cra/Justin Trudeau). **Getty Images**: Jimmy Sime / Central Press (ca). **Library and Archives Canada**: Duncan Cameron (ca/Lester B. Pearson, cra); William James Topley (tc); Notman Studio (tl); Topley Studio Fonds (tc/Robert Laird Borden); Yousuf Karsh (tr); National Film Board (cla). **60 Getty Images**: Bettmann (cb). **61 The Canadian Press**: Doug Ball (c); Peter Bregg (crb). **63 Library and Archives Canada**: (t). **66 Library and Archives Canada**: Notman Studio (cla). **67 Library and Archives Canada**: (tl). **68 Library and Archives Canada**: William James Topley (cla). **69 Library and Archives Canada**: William James Topley (cb). **70 Library and Archives Canada**: Topley Studio Fonds (cla). **71 The Canadian Press**: (bl). **72 Library and Archives Canada**: Yousuf Karsh (cla). **73 Library and Archives Canada**: (cb). **74 Library and Archives Canada**: National Film Board (cla). **75 The Canadian Press**: (bl). **76 Getty Images**: Jimmy Sime / Central Press (cla). **77 Alamy Stock Photo**: Cosmo Condina (cb). **78 Library and Archives Canada**: Duncan Cameron (cla). **79 Library and Archives Canada**: Duncan Cameron (bl). **80 Library and Archives Canada**: Duncan Cameron (cla). Rex by Shutterstock: Canadian Press (br). **81 Rex by Shutterstock**: Canadian Press (bl). **82 Alamy Stock Photo**: Tim Graham (cla). **84 Alamy Stock Photo**: Sputnik (cla). **85 Alamy Stock Photo**: Reuters (tl). Reuters: Peter Jones / Files (tr). **86 Alamy Stock Photo**: Reuters / Chris Wattie (bl); Victor Biro (cla). **87 Alamy Stock Photo**: Reuters / Adrien Veczan (tr). **88 Alamy Stock Photo**: LJ Mil (cla); Reuters / Chris Wattie (b)

Cover images: Front: **123RF.com**: tanyar30; **Getty Images**: Bettmann cb, Chung Sung-Jun crb, The Print Collector clb; **Rex by Shutterstock**: Nils Jorgensen cb/(Brian Mulroney); Back: **Rex by Shutterstock**: Canadian Press tr

All other images © Dorling Kindersley
For further information see: www.dkimages.com

A WORLD OF IDEAS:
SEE ALL THERE IS TO KNOW

www.dk.com

Contents

4   Meet the Prime Minister

6   **Chapter 1:** What is a Democracy?

16   **Chapter 2:** How does Canada's Government Work?

24   **Chapter 3:** How is Canada's Government Formed?

40   **Chapter 4:** The Government in Action!

58   **Chapter 5:** The Prime Ministers of Canada

90   Our Great Prime Ministers Quiz

92   Glossary

94   Guide for Parents

96   Index

Meet the Prime Minister

Do you recognize this face? Probably! Whether you follow politics or not, the Prime Minister is one of the most recognized people in Canada. The Prime Minister is often on the news: talking at press conferences, shaking hands with people at events across Canada, and dealing

Justin Trudeau was elected Prime Minister on October 19, 2015.

with *diplomats* abroad and with emergencies here at home.

But who, or what, is a Prime Minister, exactly? And what do Prime Ministers do?

The Prime Minister of Canada is the official leader of the Canadian government. Even so, the Prime Minister is not an absolute ruler. They can't do whatever they want!

In fact, the Prime Minister is often called "first among equals." This phrase means that even though he or she leads Canada's government, a Prime Minister doesn't lead alone. More than 300 people—elected Members of Canada's House of Commons—work together to make the *laws* that govern the daily lives of all Canadians.

Every single one of them, even the Prime Minister, must follow the same rules that every other Canadian follows. Everyone is equal. No one is "above the law."

Life of the party?

The Prime Minister is not just Canada's head of government. He or she is also the head of one of Canada's political parties. A party is a group of people that share similar ideas about how a country should be organized and run. In the House of Commons, the political party with the most elected members forms the government.

The party with the second greatest number of elected members forms the official Opposition. It's the Opposition's job to keep an eye on the government, and make sure they are doing their job properly.

The Prime Minister's job is an important one. It's also complicated. To understand it, we'll need to find out more about how Canada's government was formed, how it is structured, and how it works on a day-to-day basis.

Being the Prime Minister does come with a few perks. For example, Prime Ministers live in an official residence during their time in office. The house doesn't have a name. It's known only by its address: 24 Sussex Drive. It's in Ottawa, close to the Parliament buildings.

Another perk is that you get a fancy title. You get to be called The Right Honourable .... for the rest of your life!

(write your name here)

Words that appear in *italic text* can be found in the glossary at the back of the book on pages 92–93.

Chapter 1
What is a Democracy?

Canada's style of government is called a *parliamentary democracy*. The word *"democracy"* comes from two Greek words: "demos" (people) and "kratos" (rule). Together, they mean "rule by the people." In a democracy, the people rule! They make the decisions, not the king, queen, or any other leader.

The word "parliamentary" explains how people make those decisions. A Parliament is a group of people made up of elected Members. It makes decisions on behalf of people who vote for them—the country's citizens.

The word "parliament" comes from the French word "parler." It means "to talk." It's a perfect name, because Members of Parliament talk about new laws, decisions of government, and more.

How we got our parliamentary democracy

The roots of our system of government go back
to 1215, long before Canada existed, and to a
faraway country, England.

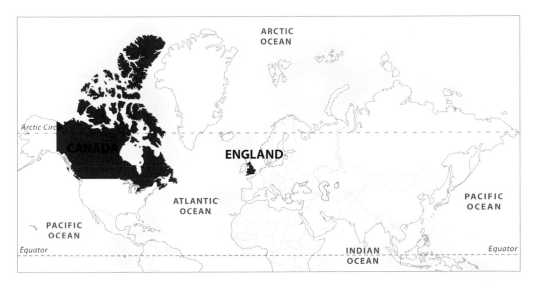

During the Middle Ages, English kings or queens could
do almost anything they wanted. They raised money by
taxing their people. If people didn't pay, they could be
thrown in jail or executed!

Some *monarchs* used their power unfairly. It caused a lot
of suffering. Things got so bad under England's King John
(1199–1216), a few nobles banded together and forced him
to sign a document giving up some power. The document,
called the Magna Carta, limited *taxes* English monarchs
could demand. It prevented them from jailing people
without good reason. It also stated that people accused
of crimes would get a trial in a reasonable amount of time
after they were charged.

King John taxed his people heavily, imprisoned his nephew, and lost England's territories in battles. He was an unpopular king!

The Magna Carta changed English government forever. From 1215 on, the English monarch no longer had absolute power. What they could do was limited by a document, or *constitution*. It acted like an instruction book, telling everyone what was allowed and what wasn't.

The new form of government was called a *constitutional monarchy.*

It's the style of government that Great Britian has today. Canada also has a constitutional monarchy. That's because Canada used to belong to Great Britain!

In 1707, England joined together with Scotland to become Great Britain.

From colony to country

In the fifteenth century, Europeans travelled all over the world. They found new lands that they didn't know about before. This included North America!

The English and the French realized they could make money from North America's timber, fish, furs, and minerals. They decided to colonize it—to claim the land for themselves (although there'd been people living there for thousands of years).

The English and French monarchs sent settlers to seize, clear, and farm the land. In return for "free" land, settlers sent taxes back to England and France.

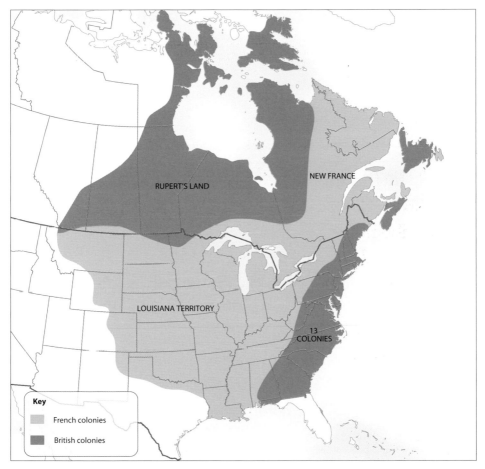

This map shows the British and French colonies in North America circa 1754. The British owned Rupert's Land, which was controlled by the Hudson's Bay Company, parts of the Maritimes, and the original 13 colonies of the United States. The French had control of New France and the Louisiana Territory. The American colonies rebelled against Britain in 1776 and became an independent country—the United States of America. France sold its Louisiana colony to the United States in 1803. The French colony of New France became a British one in 1763, at the end of the Seven Years' War.

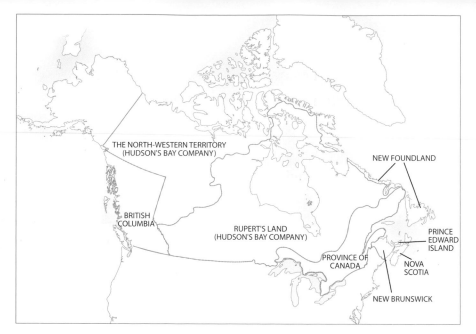
British colonies in 1867

Unrest in the colonies

By 1867, Canada was made up of several British colonies, including the Province of Canada (parts of Ontario and Quebec), New Brunswick, Nova Scotia, Prince Edward Island, Newfoundland, and British Columbia. The colonies were ruled by British Governors appointed by the British Monarch, Queen Victoria.

The Governors were mostly born and raised in Great Britain. They didn't understand the colonial settlers' concerns. They saw the colonies simply as a source of riches—for Queen Victoria, and themselves.

Confederation

The people who lived in the colonies didn't enjoy watching their hard-earned money flow out of the colonies and back to Great Britain. But each colony had little power. If they joined together, they could improve their situation.

Some of the colonies decided to form a Confederation—a union of independent territories. After three years of negotiation, the deal was done. From then on, Ontario and Quebec (formerly the Province of Canada), Nova Scotia, and New Brunswick would work together.

John A. Macdonald, the *premier* of the Ontario colony, was one of the main architects of Confederation. He became Canada's first Prime Minister.

Alexander Mackenzie was the other driving force behind Confederation. He had been a political activist and a member of the government of the Province of Canada. He became Canada's second Prime Minister.

George-Étienne Cartier was another major figure of Confederation. He was an active member of Quebec politics. He helped bring Quebec, Manitoba, the Northwest Territories, and British Columbia into Confederation.

Breaking free of Great Britain

The new Canadian Confederation still belonged to the British Empire. It couldn't do anything without permission from Great Britain! No one knew if Britain would let its Canadian colonies rule themselves without a battle.

Canadians sent representatives to London to fight for their cause. It turned out Great Britain didn't want to go to war with its Canadian colonies. On July 1, 1867, the British

Parliament passed the British North America Act (BNA Act). The Act officially created the Dominion of Canada, or Canada for short. Canada would now be able to make more of its own decisions. But more than a century would pass before Canada was completely independent.

The BNA Act also served as Canada's original Constitution. It set out the structure of the system of government we still use today. It also gave Canadians some basic rights and freedoms.

Canada Day celebrates the birth of our nation every year on July 1.

A new country

The new country needed a new government. Canada set up a *federal* government to oversee issues, such as railways and trade, that affected all the former colonies (now called provinces). It also dealt with foreign governments on their behalf.

Each province, however, kept its own provincial government. They managed the provinces' internal affairs, such as hospitals and schools.

While Canada is an independent country, it's still part of the "British Commonwealth." All Commonwealth countries have the British Monarch as their head of state. They also share similar styles of government.

Joining the party

Over time, other British colonies joined the Canadian Confederation.

When provinces and territories joined Confederation	
Ontario, Quebec, New Brunswick, Nova Scotia	1867
Manitoba, Northwest Territories	1870
British Columbia	1871
Prince Edward Island	1873
Yukon Territory	1898
Alberta, Saskatchewan	1905
Newfoundland and Labrador	1949
Nunavut*	1999

*Nunavut was part of the Northwest Territories until 1999, when it broke off to become a new territory.

The Constitution

The rules for how the new Confederation—a new country—would operate were written down in Canada's Constitution in 1867. The Constitution tells us how to hold elections, how Parliament works, and what powers the federal and provincial governments have. It also spells out the duties of the Prime Minister and the Monarch (the King or Queen).

Canada's Constitution is made up of more than 25 separate documents. These include the Charter of Rights and Freedoms, the BNA Act, and the Constitution Act of 1982.

Can we change the Constitution?

While a constitution tries to set rules for all circumstances, over time, there might be good reasons for tweaking it. A country may want to change how it holds elections, for example.

In Canada, we couldn't change our Constitution until 1982. That's because the BNA Act, the founding document of Canada, could only be changed with Great Britain's permission!

Prime Minister Pierre Trudeau and Queen Elizabeth II sign the Proclamation of the Constitution Act on April 17, 1982.

In 1982, British Parliament passed the Constitution Act. It allowed Canada to change its Constitution without Great Britain's approval. It also added the Charter of Rights and Freedoms to the Constitution. Some consider this to be the moment that Canada gained true independence.

What's up with the Queen?

Since Canada is an independent country, why do we have a Queen? For the most part, the role of the Monarch, or "Crown," is ceremonial in Canada. It's kept for the sake of tradition. For that reason, it's said that Canada's Monarch "reigns, but does not rule." The Monarch is the official Head of State in Canada and is responsible for:

- Swearing in a new Prime Minister
- Approving Senate and Judge appointments
- Opening new sessions of Parliament with the Speech from the Throne
- Closing or "dissolving" a session of Parliament
- Giving the final stamp of approval to new laws
- Representing Canada abroad
- Serving as Commander-in-Chief of Canada's armed forces
- Awarding honours and rewards
- Bestowing citizenship

Since the Queen lives in Britain and doesn't visit Canada often, her tasks in Canada are performed by the Governor General, the Queen's official representative. The Governor General also gets to live in an official residence—Rideau Hall in Ottawa.

Chapter 2

How Does Canada's Government Work?

Canada is a huge country. It spans almost 10 million square kilometres and is home to more than 35 million people. To help manage such a big country, the government is split into different divisions with different responsibilities.

Division of government

Canada has three levels of government: **federal**, **provincial**, and **municipal**. Each level has separate responsibilities and separate powers.

The **federal government** is responsible for laws and services that affect the whole country, such as collecting federal taxes, negotiating with foreign countries, providing national defence, and writing and enforcing criminal law.

It also handles citizenship, banking, the post office, employment insurance, broadcasting, and the country's budget.

The federal government is based in Ottawa, Canada's capital. It's headed by the Prime Minister (the PM for short).

Provincial/territorial governments are responsible for laws and services that affect a province or territory. These include collecting provincial taxes, overseeing schools, delivering health care, building and maintaining highways and prisons, and certifying marriages.

Provincial governments often work with the federal government on large projects. They are headed by elected Premiers.

Municipal governments are responsible for *by-laws* and services that help a city or town function—if a pothole appears in your street, your municipal government is who you would call.

Public transit in Calgary is handled by the Calgary municipal government.

They manage public transit (trains and buses), provide water and sewer services, collect garbage and recycling, maintain city streets and sidewalks, provide firefighting and police services, and maintain parks, libraries, and community centres. Municipal governments are headed by Mayors or Reeves.

In some cases, municipal services might be delivered by the provincial or federal government. For example, if a town is too small to fund their own police force, local policing might be provided by the provincial police force or the RCMP (Royal Canadian Mounted Police), the federal police force.

This is Canada's Coat of Arms. The official motto of Canada is "A Mari Usque Ad Mare." It's a Latin phrase meaning "from sea to sea."

18

The federal government

The federal government is responsible for matters affecting the whole country. That's a big job!

To do it, the government is split into three branches: Executive, Legislative, and Judicial.

The *Executive Branch* is made up of the Prime Minister and the *Cabinet*. The *Legislative Branch* is made up of the House of Commons and the Senate. The *Judicial Branch* is composed of the courts and the justice system. You will learn more about the Cabinet, the House of Commons, and the Senate in Chapter 4.

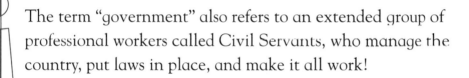

The term "government" also refers to an extended group of professional workers called Civil Servants, who manage the country, put laws in place, and make it all work!

Division of powers

It's not an accident that there are three separate branches of government. Canada's founders knew their history! They knew exactly what could happen if one person (such as England's King John) had too much power.

To guard against this, Canada's Constitution divided power among three separate branches. Each branch had a different, but equally important role. No one branch could run the country alone.

If one branch overstepped—for example, if the Prime Minister started making laws—the other two branches could join together to stop it. They could **check**—or rein in—that branch. They would provide **balance** to keep each other in line.

This system of **checks and balances** is an important form of protection for the Canadian people.

The federal government at a glance
This chart shows the three branches of the federal government, and how they relate to each other.

Monarch
(Queen/King of Great Britain),
represented in Canada by the
Governor General

PARLIAMENT

Executive Branch
- Prime Minister and the Cabinet

Legislative Branch
- The Senate
- The House of Commons

Judicial Branch
- Supreme Court of Canada
- Federal Court of Canada
- Provincial Courts

PM Justin Trudeau visits Fort McMurray, Alberta, after it was destroyed by wildfires in 2016. The federal government matched all donations to the Canadian Red Cross to help with relief efforts.

The branches of the federal government

The **Executive Branch** consists of the Prime Minister and his or her Cabinet. The Cabinet is a group of people chosen by the PM to help make decisions. Together, they introduce and pass laws, manage the government, and spend tax money. In case of a disaster, the Executive Branch helps direct and fund relief efforts.

The **Legislative Branch** consists of two parts, the Senate and the House of Commons.

The Senate (or Upper House) is made up of representatives *appointed* by the Governor General, on the advice of the Prime Minister. Senators may serve until the age of 75. There can be up to 105 senators at any time.

The House of Commons (or Lower House) is made up of representatives who have been elected by Canadian citizens. They're called *Members of Parliament*, or MPs for short.

The Senate and the House of Commons work together to propose *bills*—ideas that, if agreed upon, become law. For a bill to pass, or become law, more than half the members of both houses must vote for it.

Together, the Executive and the Legislative branches make up Canada's Parliament—the main law-making force in Canada's government.

In December 2016, there were 335 Members of Parliament and 102 Senators.

Judicial

The Judicial Branch consists of the Supreme Court, the Federal Court, and the Provincial Courts. It's in charge of *interpreting* the laws made by Parliament. The court system also decides if laws have been broken, and what the consequences might be. The Judicial Branch is kept separate from Parliament, to make sure that it remains independent and *unbiased*. Even the Prime Minister has to obey the laws and respect the court's decisions. PMs can't fire judges, either!

The Supreme Court is the highest court in Canada. It has nine judges. They interpret the Constitution and make decisions on important legal matters. They also hear *appeals* from people who aren't happy with decisions made by lower courts.

The Federal Court hears the most serious criminal cases and settles disputes between individuals and the federal government.

Provincial Courts hear less serious criminal cases and matters of provincial law.

The Royal Touch

The Monarch, as the Head of State of Canada, is not a branch of the Canadian government. Instead, it is part of every branch of the federal government. Even though the Monarch and the Monarch's representative, the Governor General, are technically "in charge," in practice, they do not play an active role in government.

Governor General Michaëlle Jean (right) greets Queen Elizabeth II during a royal visit to Canada in 2010. Queen Elizabeth II has been Canada's reigning monarch since 1952!

Chapter 3

How is Canada's Government Formed?

Becoming the Prime Minister

The Prime Minister is the leader of the Executive Branch of the Canadian government. But how do you get from "ordinary citizen" to leader of the Canadian government? It's not easy!

Your first step might be to join a political party.

It's a party

Political parties are groups of people with similar ideas about how the government and country should be run. Party members work together to get elected and to pass laws they believe are the best for the country.

In Canada, there are three major national political parties: the Liberal Party, the Conservative Party, and the New Democratic Party (NDP). There are other smaller parties and regional parties too, such as the Green Party and Bloc Québécois.

Parties are not fixed or permanent. In 1945, for example, there were 11 parties in Canada, each with members in the House of Commons!

Over time, political parties might change their names, split, disband, or merge. Today's Conservative Party of Canada, for example, came about from a merger between the Progressive Conservative and Canadian Alliance Parties. Political parties also come in all stripes. The Rhinoceros Party of Canada, active from 1963 to 1993, was formed to poke fun at the political process and to entertain voters. It once promised to repeal the law of gravity!

Forming the government

No matter what their ideas, political parties all share a common goal: to get as many members of their party elected to the House of Commons as possible. That's because the party that has the most elected members gets to form the next government. They will decide what course Canada will take by passing new laws and making new agreements with the leaders of other countries.

Even so, getting new laws made isn't easy. The government has to convince the rest of Parliament—and the country—that what they propose is the best course of action.

Prime Minister Justin Trudeau (centre) meets with US President Barack Obama (right) and Mexico's President Enrique Peña Nieto (left) in Ottawa, 2016. They met to discuss various issues and plans to benefit the three countries.

The Opposition

The party with the second greatest number of MPs elected to the House of Commons is called the Official Opposition. Its job is to challenge the government, and help ensure the laws it passes are fair, effective, and what Canadians truly want.

In 2016, the House of Commons was made up of 182 Liberal MPs, 97 Conservative, 44 NDP, 10 Bloc Québécois, 1 Green Party, and 1 Independent. The Liberals hold the most seats, so they form the government. The Conservatives have the second largest number of seats, so they form the Official Opposition. The rest of the parties are called Opposition Parties.

Parliament may also include one or more Opposition Parties. They usually work with the Official Opposition to keep an eye on the government.

From party member to party leader

If you want to become Prime Minister, you have to be elected leader of your political party. To do so, you must convince party members to vote for you in a *leadership convention*.

At the convention, party members *debate* who would be the best leader. They then hold a vote. The winner becomes the party leader, and the person who represents them in Parliament.

Prime Minister Jean Chrétien (left) congratulates Paul Martin as he is elected the new leader of the Liberal Party in 2003.

Elections 101

Congratulations! You've been voted leader of your party. You now might get a chance to become Canada's Prime Minister. That chance will come at Canada's next federal, or general, *election*.

The general election

The Canadian Constitution guarantees that elections are held on a regular basis. At the very least, elections must be held on the third Monday in October within four years of the previous election.

Prime Ministers cannot currently remain in office for longer than four years, unless they are re-elected. The longest-serving PM was William Lyon Mackenzie King. He served a total of 22 years in office from 1921 to 1930 and 1935 to 1948. The shortest-serving was Charles Tupper. He served for just 69 days in 1896.

Charles Tupper was the shortest-serving PM.

Elections, however, can take place more often than every four years. The Governor General can call an election at any time, under certain conditions. Early elections can be called on the advice of the current Prime Minister. They can also be called if the Government receives a *No Confidence* vote from the House of Commons.

A vote of No Confidence is when the majority of the House of Commons believe that the current government is no longer capable of running the country.

An election might also be held if the government can't get a budget—a spending plan for the country—approved in the House.

Who can vote?

All* Canadian citizens 18 years and older who have registered to vote can elect representatives to the House of Commons. A citizen is a person who has full legal rights to live, work, and vote in Canada. You gain Canadian citizenship if:

- You are born in Canada
- One or both of your parents are Canadian citizens
- You have lived in Canada for six years, and apply for citizenship.

*Only two people are not allowed to vote. That's the Chief Electoral Officer of Canada, the person who oversees Canadian elections, and his or her assistant.

Early in Canada's history, the right to vote was restricted. Only wealthy men could vote. If you were a woman or an indigenous person, you couldn't vote because you weren't considered a person under the law! Women got the right to vote in the federal elections in 1918. *Indigenous people got the right in 1960.*

Clockwise from top left: Lillian Beynon Thomas, Winona Dixon, Amelia Burritt, and Dr. Mary Crawford presented a petition for women's voting rights in 1915 to the Manitoba government. Manitoba was the first province in Canada to give women the right to vote in 1916, two years earlier than the federal government.

Ridings

For election purposes, Canada is divided into *ridings*. A riding is an area of the country based on population. Each riding can choose one person as its Member of Parliament.

Because ridings are based on population, they vary greatly in geographic size. For example, there are 25 separate ridings within the city of Toronto, but only one in all of Nunavut!

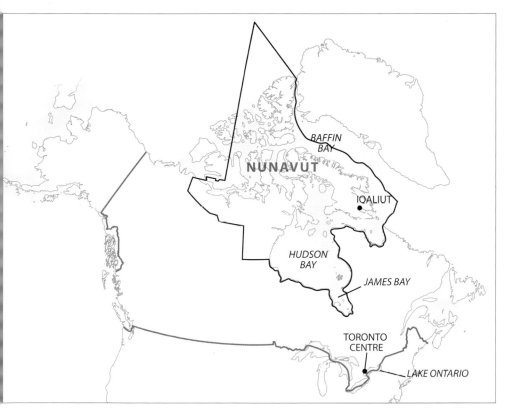

Canada's largest riding, geographically, is Nunavut. It measures approximately 2 million square kilometres, and contains about 30,000 people. Toronto Centre, one of 25 ridings in the city of Toronto, measures approximately just 6 square kilometres and contains about 94,000 people.

When an election is called, political parties draw up a list, or "slate" of candidates. Each candidate is assigned to a specific riding. The voters in that riding will then choose from among each party's candidates in that riding.

Occasionally, someone who's not a member of a party may throw their hat in the ring. They are called "Independent" candidates.

The candidate in each riding who gets the most votes wins a seat in the House of Commons, and will represent that riding in Parliament.

Once in Parliament, each MP is expected to *advocate* for the interests of the people in his or her riding. Different ridings' interests often clash. The people in a Toronto riding, for example, might want federal funding for city subways. The people in a rural riding in northern Alberta might be dead set against that, because the money will be spent on something that they will not benefit from. It's up to the new MPs to come up with plans that both benefit their ridings <u>and</u> address the needs of the country as a whole.

Party leaders have to run too!

Party leaders aren't guaranteed seats in Parliament. They also have to run for election in a riding. If their party wins a majority in the House of Commons,

they become Prime Minister!

But what if the leader doesn't win their seat? If that happens, one MP from their party usually resigns their seat. A special election, called a by-election, is then held in that riding, with the Prime Minister on the *ballot.*

Conservative leader Brian Mulroney receives a pair of running shoes at the beginning of his campaign from his staff, a joke on "running" for election!

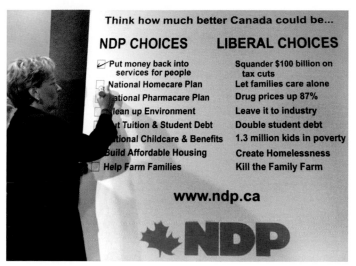

Think how much better Canada could be...

NDP CHOICES	LIBERAL CHOICES
☑ Put money back into services for people	Squander $100 billion on tax cuts
National Homecare Plan	Let families care alone
National Pharmacare Plan	Drug prices up 87%
Clean up Environment	Leave it to industry
Cut Tuition & Student Debt	Double student debt
National Childcare & Benefits	1.3 million kids in poverty
Build Affordable Housing	Create Homelessness
Help Farm Families	Kill the Family Farm

www.ndp.ca

NDP

In 2000, NDP leader Alexa McDonough explains how her party's election promises compare to the Liberal Party's.

On the campaign trail

The weeks leading up to an election are known as "campaign season." During this time, political parties compete to convince voters that their vision for Canada is the best. Each candidate's task is to persuade voters in their riding that they, and their party, are the best representative for that riding. They encourage people to vote for them by sharing their party's *platform*—its views and promises—in an exciting way.

Campaign season generally lasts about a month. If parties sense an election is about to be called, it can start earlier.

During campaign season, the leaders of the political parties work non-stop! They take part in TV debates, arguing over issues like health care, education, taxes, and foreign *policy*. The would-be MPs also take part in smaller debates in their ridings.

To encourage people to vote for them, candidates aim to meet as many of their riding's *constituents*—the people who live in the riding—as possible. They may host community events like barbecues where they make their case. They may knock on doors to speak to voters, hand out flyers at malls, or hold meetings to discuss issues.

Because parties need money to run a campaign, some of these events will also be fundraisers. If you strongly support a candidate, you might donate money to help him or her win! This money is used for things such as advertising, paying staff, and travel.

Prime Minister Paul Martin flips burgers at a community barbecue as he campaigns for re-election in 2004.

The dark side of campaigning

Sir John A. Macdonald, Canada's first Prime Minister, once said, "If you would know the depth of meanness of human nature, you have got to be a Prime Minister running a general election."

Macdonald meant that campaigning frequently brings out the worst in people. It's a competition, and not everyone plays fair. Some candidates might bribe—pay money to—voters for their votes. They might take money illegally from unions or businesses that hope to influence them. They may try to fool their opponents' voters by giving them wrong information about where or when the voting will take place. They might even steal or destroy ballots that aren't in their favour, or "stuff the ballot box" with phony ballots that are.

Elections Canada is the agency that supervises the election process. It tries to make sure everyone follows the rules. If candidates or party officials are caught doing something wrong during the campaign, they can go to jail.

To help keep things fair, Elections Canada provides some funding to political parties for their campaigns. It also limits how much money larger parties can spend, so they don't get an unfair advantage over smaller parties with less money.

On the attack

In general, candidates try to present their platforms in the best possible light. But sometimes, they don't stick to this tactic and attack their opponents instead. They may create TV ads or social media campaigns designed to make the other side look foolish or criminal.

Sometimes attack ads work. Other times they backfire. In 1993, the Progressive Conservative Party ran a TV ad that seemed to make fun of Liberal Party leader Jean Chrétien's partial facial paralysis, caused by Bell's palsy. The ad asked "Is this a Prime Minister?" Voters were angry, the ad was pulled, but the damage was done—the Progressive Conservatives lost the election to the Liberals.

During the 1979 federal election, Progressive Conservative candidate Joe Clark attacked his opponent, the then

Prime Minister Pierre Trudeau. He said, "A recession is when your neighbour loses his job. A depression is when you lose your job. Recovery is when Pierre Trudeau loses his job." Clark won the election.

Election day!

The big day has arrived. Each riding sets up "polling stations." These are places registered voters go to vote for their chosen candidate. Each riding has several polling stations (or "polls") so voters won't have to travel far to reach one.

Polls are usually open from early morning to late evening. Employers are required by law to give their workers enough time before, after, or during their shifts to get to the polls.

········ ABOUD, Emran ········
·· New Democratic Party of Canada ··

········ CHOW, Elizabeth ········
········ Green Party of Canada ·······

········ EVANS, Sandra ········
···· Conservative Party of Canada ····

······ LALONDE, Philippe ······
······ Liberal Party of Canada ······

The ballot for a federal election is a piece of paper printed with candidates' names and the party they belong to. Voters mark their choice.

What if you can't make it to the polls on Election Day? You can still vote. People can vote ahead of time in advance polls. They can also apply for a "special ballot" that will let them mail in their vote from anywhere in the world.

Completed ballots are folded so that the voter's choice is not visible. It's then deposited into a sealed ballot box under the watchful eye of Elections Canada officials. After the polling station closes, ballots are counted under careful supervision. The results from each polling station are added together to determine the winner in each riding.

In Canada, the law says that all voting must be done in secret, and that nobody can force you to share the details of who or which party you voted for. This rule prevents employers or landlords from pressuring you to vote a certain way to keep your job or home, or people paying for other's votes.

Prime Minister Stephen Harper votes (probably for himself!) in a privacy booth in the 2015 general election.

And the winner is....

The candidates in each riding with the most votes are awarded seats in the House of Commons. They now become Members of Parliament.

Majority vs. minority

The party with the most candidates elected to the House of Commons is declared the winner overall. It is invited to form the new government by the Governor General.

If it won more than half of the seats in the House of Commons, it will form a "majority government." If it won less than half, it will form a "minority government."

Majority governments are more powerful than minority governments. For a bill to pass in the House of Commons, it needs "yes" votes from half of the MPs plus one additional vote. Since they have enough members to win any vote, majority governments can accomplish more of their goals

A poster outside Prime Minister Pierre Trudeau's office makes fun of his minority government's unstable position in 1972.

without having to compromise, or needing to convince members of the opposition to support their policies.

Minority governments, on the other hand, must get the support of some of the opposition to pass new laws.

Majority governments usually survive longer than minority ones. This is because minority governments are more likely to receive a vote of No Confidence over an important proposal, such as the country's budget. They simply don't have enough power to push it through. If that happens, a new election will be called.

Coalition!

Imagine this: a new minority government has just been formed. But if this new government joins with one of the smaller opposition parties, they'd have more than half of the seats and could form a majority government, called a *coalition* government. This makes the government stronger, but the smaller party gains too. It might demand that some of its ideas are adopted by the larger party in exchange for its support. If its wishes aren't met, it could pull out of the coalition and vote against the government.

Coalition governments can be very effective, especially if the political parties that form them have similar points of view. But they have been very rare in Canadian history. Why? It can be tricky to form a coalition. If each party had ideas so similar to each other that they can get along without friction, they wouldn't be separate parties, would they?

Chapter 4
The Government in Action!

Now that you have fought and won a long campaign season and election, it is time to begin governing as Prime Minister. Many people depend on you to make decisions to improve their lives. They may be much like you and could have voted for you, or they may be very different from you and disagree with you. As Prime Minister it is your job to help them all.

Isn't this job too big for one person?

Yes. Luckily, Prime Ministers don't have to do it alone. They have three separate groups of people to help and advise them: the Cabinet, the House of Commons, and the Senate. In this chapter, we'll take a look at these groups and how they all work together to form Canada's Parliament, and also at some of the key roles of the Prime Minister and his or her government.

The Cabinet

The Cabinet is a small group of people hand-picked by the Prime Minister. Cabinet Ministers are usually Members of Parliament; sometimes they are senators. While they don't have to be, they are usually members of the PM's own party.

Cabinet Ministers are each assigned a "portfolio," or department, to oversee. Ideally, they will be people with broad experience in that area. Portfolios include key areas such as Finance, Foreign Affairs, Energy, Housing, Indigenous and Northern Affairs, Justice, and Defence.

Cabinet Ministers are addressed with special titles that reflect their portfolios. The Minister in charge of Finance, for example, is called the Minister of Finance.

Each portfolio is also assigned to one or more members of the Opposition Parties by their leaders. It's their job to keep an eye on the government and hold it accountable for its actions. Together, these Opposition members are referred to as the Shadow Cabinet.

Shadow Cabinet members are each referred to as a "critic." For example, the Shadow Cabinet member who looks after Justice is called the "justice critic."

Choosing the Cabinet

It is not easy to select an effective Cabinet. Prime Ministers will look at how much experience each person has before making a choice. For example, is the potential Finance Minister a former banker, or an economist? The PM will also consider how much influence their potential Cabinet members have within the party and what province they are from.

Finally, the PM will look at gender, ethnicity, and other personal factors. A cabinet that reflects the *diversity* of Canada's citizens insures everyone's perspective will be heard.

Half of Prime Minister Justin Trudeau's Cabinet in 2015 is made up of women, a first for Canada.

The House of Commons

The House of Commons is made up of Members of Parliament elected by Canadians. As Prime Minister, you cannot govern without the approval of the House of Commons. If most MPs decide that they don't support you as Prime Minister, you might be out of a job.

For example, if Parliament supports a No Confidence motion, you will have to fight another election to regain

Members of Parliament in action in the House of Commons.

the Prime Minister's Office. To avoid this, the Prime Minister must keep the House of Commons on his or her side.

The House of Commons is often called the "Lower House" because its members must fight for re-election every few years. The MPs who make up the House of Commons come from all walks of life. Some are former professionals, some are activists or community leaders, and some can even be students!

The Senate

The Senate is the "Upper House" in Parliament. Unlike MPs, senators are appointed instead of elected. The Governor General makes appointments on the advice of the Prime Minister.

Senators represent all regions of Canada. They may serve until they are 75 years old.

Since senators don't have to run for election, they are (in theory!) less influenced by party politics than MPs.

This chart shows how many senators represented each region of Canada in 2016.

Number of senators	Province
6	Alberta
6	British Columbia
5	Manitoba
10	New Brunswick
6	Newfoundland and Labrador
1	Northwest Territories
9	Nova Scotia
1	Nunavut
24	Ontario
4	Prince Edward Island
23	Quebec
6	Saskatchewan
1	Yukon
Total: 102	

The Senate supports and advises the Prime Minister. It helps pass new laws. It reviews bills passed by the House of Commons. It also proposes bills. Both the Senate and the House of Commons need to pass, or approve, a bill for it to become law.

Most bills originate in the House of Commons, but the Senate can propose new bills as well.

The Senate can also set up committees that study important issues like health care, unemployment, aging, the military, and education. Senators make recommendations to the other parts of government about how to improve their policies.

Meeting and more meetings

The Prime Minister, Members of the Cabinet, Members of Parliament, and senators all have to attend many meetings while Parliament is in session. There are regular sittings of Parliament that happen every day, committee meetings to look at specific issues or problems, and caucus meetings, which are private meetings of all the MPs from a particular political party.

Question Period

Although it only lasts about 45 minutes, Question Period is probably the most important part of the day on Parliament Hill. During this time, Members of Parliament get to question, and hold to account, the Prime Minister and his or her Cabinet Ministers. The Opposition asks them to explain or accept responsibility for their decisions and policies. The government has to defend them. The questions asked are usually about the most important and controversial issues of the day.

Question Period can be intense and full of drama. To keep everything in line, Question Period follows a set of rules, just like every other part of Parliament. The Official Opposition begins by asking—and getting answers to—

Catherine McKenna, the Environment Minister, gets applause from her fellow Liberal party members after speaking in Question Period in 2016.

three questions. It can follow up with two more questions. Afterwards every other opposition party, in order of the number of seats they hold, may ask two questions. Finally, individual MPs may ask two questions.

Question Period is often broadcast on live TV and during the nightly news. If the government is unable to answer the questions well, it could lose support from the general public.

Parliamentarians gone wild!

MPs are not always on their best behaviour when in parliament. When tempers flare, anger can get the best of even the most level-headed MPs or PMs. In 2016,

PM Justin Trudeau dragged a member of the opposition back to his seat so that a vote could be taken. While doing this, he also accidentally elbowed another MP!

Canadian Parliament was even rowdier in the past. Canada's first PM Sir John A. Macdonald was well known for using his fists to settle disputes with other MPs and sometimes even members of the audience!

By tradition, the width of the aisle between the two sides of the House of Commons (3.96 metres) is approximately two swords' length. Sometimes, that's not far enough.

John Baird, Minister of Foreign Affairs in PM Stephen Harper's government, was known for his lively arguments in Parliament.

The Prime Minister and the Premiers

The Prime Minister meets regularly with the Premiers of the provinces and makes sure they work together. Since each Premier only represents their province, it can be easy for them to forget that their interests are not necessarily the interests of Canada as a whole.

PMs, on the other hand, represent all of Canada. They cannot favour one province over the others. But they must make sure each Premier feels like their province's needs are being taken seriously.

Prime Minister Stephen Harper meets with Alberta Premier Ed Stelmach to tour the fire-damaged areas of Slave Lake in 2011.

Laying down the law

A major part of the PM's job is proposing new laws.

Laws are the rules you and others have to live by. Some laws are good for everyone, such as the law against stealing from or hurting someone else. The reasons for other laws is not always obvious. For example, in Petrolia, Ontario, there used to be a law that made it illegal for people to whistle!

Making or repealing (getting rid of) laws is a long process. It involves the Prime Minister, the Cabinet, the House of Commons, the Senate, and the Governor General.

Step one

Before a law becomes a law, it is called a "bill." A bill describes whom the law would affect, what it would do, and how it would be enforced.

A new bill usually starts with the Prime Minister and the Cabinet. They focus on a problem and decide how to fix it. When they write the bill, they consider all possible consequences and other possible points of view. The bill's language must be precise; one wrongly worded sentence can cause an otherwise desirable bill to fail.

Once the Cabinet has agreed on the contents and the wording, the bill is introduced to the House of Commons.

There are always two versions of a bill—one in English and the other in French.

Step two

When a bill is introduced, it's given a name. The first bill submitted to the House of Commons in every session is named C-1; every bill after that is numbered 2, 3, 4, etc.

Once a bill is introduced, it goes through three "readings." It will literally be read and/or summarized before the House of Commons so all of the members may understand it.

After the second reading, MPs can debate the ideas of the bill. They can suggest amendments, or changes, to it.

Some amendments might be suggested because the bill contains a mistake, or because MPs disagree with its purpose. Amendments can be minor, or they can cause major changes to its contents. After the second reading, the bill also gets sent to a committee for review. The committee studies it in detail and writes a report explaining its findings. It also suggests possible changes. The report is presented to the House. MPs can vote yes or no to any of the proposed changes.

The revised bill is then read for a third time.

After the third reading, MPs vote on the bill. If a majority vote to support it, the bill moves on to step three: Approval in the Senate.

Members of Parliament from the Conservative Party vote in the House of Commons on amendments to a bill in 2012.

Step three

The Senate is called a place of "sober second thought." Its job is to think about everything carefully and calmly. It can put the brakes on, or make changes to, a bill that might have been passed when people were over-excited, or that didn't consider the views of *minority groups*.

Each bill introduced in the Senate starts with a letter— in this case, S—and is numbered in order of the date it was introduced.

Like MPs, Senators also read bills three times, amending them after the second reading and a committee report, and voting on them after the third.

In Canada today, the Senate hardly ever changes or rejects a bill. Most Canadians would be upset if unelected officials overturned the work of the elected House of Commons.

Once the Senate approves a bill, it is sent onto its final stop, the Governor General's desk.

Step four

The bill has been passed by the House of Commons and the Senate. Now, the Governor General gives Royal Assent by signing it. The bill becomes law.

Or not! The Governor General can withhold Royal Assent by refusing to sign the bill. If this happens, the bill won't become law. Royal Assent is almost never refused though. It's a formality, a "stamp of approval."

Once signed, the bill becomes a fully binding law that can change the lives of millions of Canadians.

Governor General David Johnston (centre) participates in a Royal Assent ceremony in the Senate chamber in 2013.

Taxes

Passing laws, enforcing them, and providing services costs billions of dollars every year! Police, firefighters, doctors, and other civil servants all have to be paid. But who pays them?

You do. Through federal, provincial, and municipal taxes, Canadians pay for the public services our governments provide.

Taxes are fees a government charges to raise money to pay for services they provide. The fees are charged in different ways, and to different people within the community. Consider these common types of tax:

- **Sales Tax**: Whenever you buy something, you pay a tax on that transaction. The tax is normally a percentage of the total amount. The federal government collects sales tax on most purchases. Most provinces also charge a separate, additional sales

In Ontario, people pay 13% HST on many purchases.

tax. In some provinces the two taxes are combined into a single tax called the Harmonized Sales Tax (HST).

- **Income Tax**: The federal government taxes the total earnings, or income, that Canadians and Canadian residents make at work. People who earn more money are taxed at a higher rate than those who make less.

- **Luxury Tax**: Some items, like liquor, cigars, and very expensive homes, are considered "luxuries." Since you don't need them to survive, they are given additional taxes. Luxury taxes can also discourage people from buying harmful products, such as cigarettes.

- **Property Tax**: If you own a house or land, chances are you'll pay tax on it. The amount you pay depends on how much property you own and where it's located.

Taxes are important, but also controversial. No one likes to pay taxes! And everyone has an opinion on how those taxes should be spent by the government. It's no wonder taxes are always an important political issue.

The government operates many necessary, and popular, programs. These include employment insurance, health care, assistance to the poor, emergency services, and public transportation. Each one is funded by taxes.

The PM, the Constitution, and the Charter of Rights and Freedoms

Another important job for the Prime Minister is to protect the Constitution of Canada. A key part of Canada's Constitution is the Charter of Rights and Freedoms. It became part of the Constitution in 1982.

The Charter guarantees basic freedoms for all Canadians. These include the freedom to:

- follow your own beliefs (your conscience and your religion)
- express your opinions (in thought and expression)
- meet with anyone you choose (called "peaceful assembly and association").

It also guarantees:

- democratic rights (the right to vote)
- mobility rights (the right to move freely in and out of Canada)
- legal rights (the right to a fair trial, and to not be arrested without evidence)
- equality rights (fair treatment no matter race, ethnicity, religion, sex, age, mental or physical ability or disability)
- official language rights (the right to deal with the government in either French or English).

Notwithstanding Clause

The Notwithstanding Clause is the most controversial part of the Charter of Rights and Freedoms. This Clause allows the federal or provincial governments to make laws that go against some of the rights guaranteed in the charter. It was included because the provincial governments feared that the charter would grant too much power to the court systems and prevent the governments from making the laws they wanted.

Any laws that use the Notwithstanding Clause are only valid for five years at a time. They will then need to be reviewed and pass through the approval process again. Certain rights and freedoms can't be overruled by the Notwithstanding Clause, including the right to vote, the right to move freely, certain education and language rights, and equality between men and women.

Can you spare some change?

It is also the Prime Minister's job to make sure that the Constitution benefits the greatest number of Canadians. To do this it must be changed sometimes. That's never an easy task. Two-thirds of the provinces must agree on any proposed changes.

Sir John A. Macdonald, our first Prime Minister, wrote the original Constitution in 1867. Since then, it has been changed many times. The most recent change was in 1982. That's when then Prime Minister Pierre Trudeau repatriated the Constitution from Britain. From that date on, Canada no longer needed to get approval from Great Britain for any future changes to the Canadian Constitution.

The most recent attempts to change the Constitution took place under the leadership of Prime Minister Brian Mulroney (1984–1993). Both attempts failed. Here's what happened:

When Pierre Trudeau repatriated the Constitution from Britain in 1982, the rules stated that if two-thirds of the provinces representing at least fifty percent of the Canadian population agreed to it, they could change the Constitution. In this case, the proposed changes included putting the Constitution completely under Canadian control, and adding in the Charter of Rights and Freedoms.

This rule looked good on paper, but it had a fatal flaw: because more people lived in Ontario than anywhere else in Canada, Ontario would end up with more power than any other province. Quebec felt like they were being treated unfairly. They wanted to have the right to veto, or block, any future Constitutional changes.

Quebec refused to sign the Constitution to approve the changes, but since they didn't have enough power to block the changes, the Constitution was repatriated without their consent.

When Brian Mulroney became Prime Minister, he tried to convince Quebec, his home province, to sign the new

A protest sign against the Meech Lake Accord shows the unhappiness felt by some English-speaking Canadians.

Constitution. In 1987, he proposed an accord, or agreement, between the federal and provincial governments to address Quebec's concerns.

The Meech Lake Accord recognized Quebec as a "distinct society" and promised Quebec a special position in Canada. It also gave more power to the provincial governments. The Accord failed in 1990 when Manitoba and Newfoundland refused to approve it. The Accord was also unpopular with the voting public. Many saw it as a "backroom deal"—meaning the politicians who wrote it hadn't consulted regular Canadians about it. Others did not like that Quebec would get special treatment.

The Mulroney government tried again in 1992 with yet another agreement—the Charlottetown Accord. This deal would have been even more far-reaching than the Meech Lake Accord. In addition to recognizing Quebec as a distinct society, it would have given even more power to the provinces, and made changes to the Supreme Court, the House of Commons, and the Senate. It also promised self-government for Canada's Indigenous peoples. This time, the Accord received approval from the federal and all provincial governments, but the Mulroney government decided to put the Accord to a national *referendum*, or a special vote, to make sure that the Canadian public approved of the new deal. To pass, the Accord needed a "yes" vote from more than 50 percent of the population. It only got 46 percent.

To date, Quebec has still not signed Canada's 1982 Constitution.

Chapter 5

The Prime Ministers of Canada

R. B. Bennett was a millionaire businessman. Wilfrid Laurier came from a farming family in small-town Quebec. Alexander Mackenzie started out as a stonemason. Robert Borden was a schoolmaster.

Canada's Prime Ministers have come from all walks of life. The only definite requirement is that you must speak both French and English! The more experience and expertise you have, however, the more likely it is you will become Prime Minister.

Sir Wilfrid Laurier was the seventh Prime Minister (1896–1911) but the first French-Canadian to hold office. This was despite the fact that almost half of Canada was French-speaking at the time.

One of the most common routes to the PM's office is through the practice of law. Nineteen Prime Ministers have either studied law or worked as lawyers.

Why law? Legal training is useful if you want to help make laws. It also sharpens critical thinking skills and the ability to build a strong case in support of your position on any issue.

Legal knowledge is not the only skill useful for the job. The PM needs many talents to run Canada successfully.

Do you dream of becoming the Prime Minister one day? A good way to get started on your journey is to get involved in student government at your school, or join the youth club of the political party of your choice.

In the spotlight

To begin with, Prime Ministers need to be comfortable with 24/7 attention. Everything they say and do is caught by video cameras or microphones. Thanks to social media, any mistake can travel around the world very quickly. One slip of the tongue and they will be in hot water for days!

The most successful PMs are able to grab hold of this attention and thrive in it.

On the world stage

The Prime Minister must also represent Canada to the world. It's a key part of the job to promote Canada's interests and defend its position in the world.

With this goal in mind, the PM travels frequently to meet other world leaders. Some will be friends and allies. Others may be rivals, or even declared enemies. In either case, PMs must possess strong people skills and self-control. Even if the Prime Minister dislikes another leader or politician, he or she must always be able to put personal interests and feelings second to those of Canada as a whole.

In 2009 at the G-20 summit (a meeting of leaders from 20 countries around the world), Prime Minister Stephen Harper missed the group photograph! It was very embarrassing because it wasted the time of 19 of the world's most powerful leaders, who now had to retake the photo.

It was common knowledge that Prime Minister John Diefenbaker (1957–1963; right) and US President John F. Kennedy did not like each other. Many Canadians worried that this would get in the way of agreements that would improve the lives of Canadians.

Trudeaumania

Prime Minister Pierre Trudeau (1968–1979; 1980–1984) loved the spotlight. He used the media in a way no PM before him had ever done. He slid down stair banisters. He drove flashy sports cars. He even did fancy dance steps at Buckingham Palace!

Pierre Trudeau does a quick pirouette behind Queen Elizabeth II in 1977.

Trudeau's sharp wit delighted—and sometimes dismayed—Canadians. Either way, they could not get enough of him. The wave of popular support it earned him was nicknamed "Trudeaumania."

The brand-new Prime Minister runs away from fans as he heads into the Parliament buildings in 1968.

Responsibility

Canadians often see the Prime Minister as being personally responsible for everything that goes wrong in the country. For that reason, PMs must be ready to take the blame for almost anything that happens during their time in office. Sometimes they even have to accept responsibility for things that went wrong before they were elected, or are at least partly out of their control, such as the state of the world economy. If the economy is doing poorly, for example, the Prime Minister will often lose the next election.

This actually happened during the Great Depression (1929–1939)—twice! The US stock market crashed in 1929, causing a widespread economic crisis and massive unemployment. Its ill effects spilled over into Canada, costing millions of Canadians their life savings and their jobs, and kicking off a time of hardship and unrest known as the Dirty Thirties. As a result, Prime Minister W. L. Mackenzie King lost the general election in 1930 to Conservative Party leader R. B. Bennett, who promised to end unemployment or "perish in the attempt."

Once in office, Bennett tried various ways to help the economy. He gave the provinces millions of dollars for relief programs. He also created unpopular work camps for single unemployed men, paying them 20 cents a day—a small salary, even for the time!—for hard labour such as clearing bush and building roads.

Nothing he did helped the worsening crisis. Five years later, the economy was still doing badly. With another election looming, Bennett proposed a "new deal," which

During the Depression, many people who were too poor to buy gas would hitch their cars up to horses. These horse-drawn cars were known as "Bennett buggies."

promised unemployment insurance, a minimum wage, and help for farmers. But it was too late—more than one in four Canadians were without a job, and they were furious. In the 1935 general election, they re-elected King in a landslide victory to replace Bennett. King had successfully campaigned with the slogan "King or Chaos!"

Prime Ministers have to be able to solve problems, or at least look like they're solving them, to remain popular.

Scandal

Prime Ministers need to maintain a squeaky-clean reputation if they hope to govern well. Otherwise, a scandal might prevent them from doing their job and lead to them losing their position.

A scandal is when the government or a political party is caught doing something illegal or something that Canadians think is wrong. Often scandals involve someone in the government hiding information from Canadians, taking unfair advantage of their position, or misusing taxpayer's money.

Politicians caught in scandals are often unable to continue a life in politics because voters no longer trust them. This can bring down the government, or cause years of problems for both their party and the country as a whole.

During the 1990s, for example, the Liberal Party got into trouble when the government misused money that was meant to promote the idea of a unified Canada in Quebec. Much of the money was inappropriately paid to friends and relatives of Liberal Party members. The so-called Sponsorship Scandal took years to run its course. It eventually led to the defeat of Paul Martin's Liberal government by Stephen Harper's Conservative Party in 2006.

Meet the Prime Ministers

All of the Prime Ministers of Canada have made important contributions to Canada—both good and bad. Some have led the country through times of war and poverty. Others have successfully governed in times of peace and wealth. Whatever the case, all of Canada's Prime Ministers aimed to improve the lives of Canadians and Canada's relationship with the rest of the world.

In this section, you'll get to read brief profiles of some of Canada's best-known Prime Ministers.

Prime Minister	Party	Term
John A. Macdonald	Conservative	July 1, 1867–Nov. 5, 1873
Alexander Mackenzie	Liberal	Nov. 7, 1873–Oct. 8, 1878
John A. Macdonald	Conservative	Oct. 17, 1878–June 6, 1891
John Abbott	Conservative	June 16, 1891–Nov. 24, 1892
John Thompson	Conservative	Dec. 5, 1892–Dec. 12, 1894
Mackenzie Bowell	Conservative	Dec. 21, 1894–Apr. 27, 1896
Charles Tupper	Conservative	May 1, 1896–July 8, 1896
Wilfrid Laurier	Liberal	July 11, 1896–Oct. 6, 1911
Robert Borden	Conservative, Unionist	Oct. 10, 1911–July 10, 1920
Arthur Meighen	Unionist	July 10, 1920–Dec. 29, 1921
William Lyon Mackenzie King	Liberal	Dec. 29, 1921–June 28, 1926
Arthur Meighen	Conservative	June 29, 1926–Sept. 25, 1926
William Lyon Mackenzie King	Liberal	Sept. 25, 1926–Aug. 7, 1930
Richard B. Bennett	Conservative	Aug. 7, 1930–Oct. 23, 1935
William Lyon Mackenzie King	Liberal	Oct. 23, 1935–Nov. 15, 1948
Louis St. Laurent	Liberal	Nov. 15, 1948–June 21, 1957
John Diefenbaker	Progressive Conservative	June 21, 1957–Apr. 22, 1963
Lester Pearson	Liberal	Apr. 22, 1963–Apr. 20, 1968
Pierre Trudeau	Liberal	Apr. 20, 1968–June 3, 1979
Joe Clark	Progressive Conservative	June 4, 1979–March 2, 1980
Pierre Trudeau	Liberal	March 3, 1980–June 30, 1984
John Turner	Liberal	June 30, 1984–Sept. 17, 1984
Brian Mulroney	Progressive Conservative	Sept. 17, 1984–June 25, 1993
Kim Campbell	Progressive Conservative	June 25, 1993–Nov. 3, 1993
Jean Chrétien	Liberal	Nov. 4, 1993–Dec. 12, 2003
Paul Martin	Liberal	Dec. 12, 2003–Feb. 6, 2006
Stephen Harper	Conservative	Feb. 6, 2006–Nov. 4, 2015
Justin Trudeau	Liberal	Nov. 4, 2015–present

Sir John A. Macdonald
Canada's First Prime Minister

Party: Conservative
Home Province: Ontario
Previous Career: Lawyer
Years in Office: 1867–1873
1878–1891

Sir John A. Macdonald was one of the initiators of the Confederation and Canada's first Prime Minister. His family were Scottish immigrants who lived in Kingston, Ontario.

After finishing his education, Macdonald trained as a lawyer. He began work in Kingston, where he successfully defended a man accused of participating in the 1837 rebellion in Upper Canada.

In 1844, Macdonald was elected to the government of the Province of Canada. He quickly became one of the leading figures of the time. He remained active in Canadian politics for the next 20 years.

After Confederation, Macdonald was named Prime Minister. His government was defeated in 1873 when he was involved in a scandal—he and members of his party took bribes during the building of the Canadian Pacific Railway.

Despite the stain on his reputation, Macdonald was elected Prime Minister again 1878. He remained in power until his death in 1891.

Milestones:

- Brought Manitoba, British Columbia, Prince Edward Island, and the Northwest Territories into Canada
- Supported the building of the Canadian Pacific Railway, connecting eastern Canada with British Columbia
- Introduced the "Chinese head tax" to Canada's immigration policy

An election campaign poster for John A. Macdonald from 1891.

The "Chinese head tax" was a fee that every Chinese person entering Canada had to pay from 1885 to 1923. This was a racist policy designed to prevent Chinese people from entering Canada. In 2006, Prime Minister Stephen Harper offered a formal apology for the head tax.

Louis Riel, a Métis leader, led a rebellion against the Canadian government in western Canada. He was eventually caught and executed in public in 1885 on Macdonald's insistence. This created the beginnings of a longstanding division in Canada, between French society and English society.

Sir Wilfrid Laurier
The Great Politician

Party: Liberal
Home Province: Quebec
Previous Career: Newspaper Editor and Lawyer
Years in Office: 1896–1911
Sir Wilfrid Laurier is considered one of Canada's greatest politicians. He was Prime Minister for the longest consecutive term in Canadian history. He was also the first French-Canadian Prime Minister of Canada. He fought fiercely for the rights of the French-speaking people in Canada, yet he also worked to create a united Canada.

Wilfrid left home at the age of 11 to study in a neighbouring village. It was home to many immigrants from Scotland. There, he learned both the English language and the culture and customs of the British people. This would help him in his career in politics.

Laurier is best known for a key series of compromises made between the English- and the French-speaking parts of Canada. The biggest conflict between these two groups involved whether or not to support the British Empire and its wars. For example, most English Canadians wanted to fully support Britain in the Boer War, while French Canadians mostly wanted nothing to do with it. Laurier struck a deal: Canada would pay for the cost of weapons and transportation for Canadians who volunteered to fight for Britain. Canadian regiments, however, would not be sent to fight. This compromise and others like it reduced conflict between the two groups. It fostered national unity. It also earned Laurier the nickname "The Great Conciliator"— which means a person who is good at resolving conflict.

Milestones:
- Brought Yukon Territory, Alberta, and Saskatchewan into Canada
- Created the Canadian Navy

Laurier's former residence was also the home of Prime Minister Alexander Mackenzie. It is now a museum operated by the National Parks Service.

Sir Robert Borden
Wartime Warden

Party: Conservative
Home Province: Nova Scotia
Previous Career: Lawyer and Teacher
Years in Office: 1911–1920

Robert Borden grew up on a farm in Nova Scotia. His mother taught him how to read, and at the age of nine he went to a local village school where he did well in languages. By the time he turned 14, his studying paid off—he got a job as an assistant school master! He later became a full school master, and then a lawyer—a career he learned without attending law school.

Borden's time as Prime Minister was dominated by World War I, which began in 1914. At that time, Canada was still part of the British Empire. So when Great Britain declared war on Germany, Canada was automatically at war too!

Borden became an active supporter of the war effort and the troops. He introduced conscription—forcing men who were eligible to join the army—in 1917. This move made many people in Quebec very angry because they did not want to be forced to fight in what they saw as an English conflict. This furthered the division between French and English Canada that is still ongoing today.

After introducing conscription, Borden approached the Liberal party about forming a coalition government to help strengthen his position. Liberal leader Wilfred Laurier was against both conscription and forming a coalition, but Borden managed to arrange the union without his support. His Union government, made up of Conservatives, Liberals, and Independents who were for conscription, was elected with a large majority in December 1917. When the war ended in 1918, many Union members returned their original parties—but the Union government stayed in power until after Borden retired in 1920.

Milestones:

- Expanded the right to vote to include women who were married or related to soldiers
- Introduced the first income tax in Canada
- Moved Canada toward greater independence from the British Empire by signing the Treaty of Versailles and joining the League of Nations as a separate country

The Treaty of Versailles was the peace *treaty* that ended World War I. The League of Nations was an early version of the United Nations.

Prime Minister Robert Borden appeals to the public in Ottawa to buy Victory War Bonds to help fund the war effort.

William Lyon Mackenzie King
The Supernaturalist

Party: Liberal
Home Province: Ontario
Previous Career: Civil Servant
Years in Office: 1921–1926
 1926–1930
 1935–1948

William Lyon Mackenzie King is Canada's longest serving Prime Minister. He was in office for a total of 22 years! He led Canada into and out of the Great Depression and through World War II. King spent most of his time in office trying to reform labour laws and increase Canada's influence in the world.

When Britain declared war on Germany in 1939, King refused to join the war until after Canadian Parliament voted to do so. During the war, King served as a link between Great Britain and the United States, hosting the leaders of both countries several times in Canada. He also made sure Canada provided important aid in troops and supplies to the war effort, without resorting to conscription until later in the war.

King was in some ways an unusual person. He remained attached to his mother and his dog, even after their deaths. King believed that he could contact them in the spirit world. He used psychic mediums and Ouija boards to talk to them.

Milestones:

- Laid the groundwork for Newfoundland to join Canada
- Introduced welfare programs such as unemployment insurance and old age pension
- Initiated the creation of internment camps for Canadians of Japanese descent during World War II (when Canada was at war with Japan). Because of this racist policy, thousands of Japanese-Canadians lost their liberty and property. In 1988, PM Brian Mulroney formally apologized to Canadians who had been harmed by this injustice.

Japanese families were rounded up and sent to internment camps in British Columbia in 1942.

Louis St. Laurent
Canada's Favourite "Uncle"

Party: Liberal
Home Province: Quebec
Previous Career: Lawyer
Years in Office: 1948–1957

"Uncle" Louis St. Laurent took over the Prime Minister's office from King in 1948. He earned the nickname "Uncle Louis" on the campaign trail because Canadians saw him as a kindly uncle. He was the second French-Canadian to lead the government, and the fact that he was fluently bilingual helped to win the support of both French and English Canadians. During his time in office, Canada was one of the richest countries in the world.

St. Laurent continued King's policies of promoting Canada on the world stage. Under his leadership, Canada became a founding member of the North Atlantic Treaty Organization (NATO), an alliance of countries that aimed to prevent the spread of communism.

When the communist nation of North Korea invaded the democratic South Korea in 1950, St. Laurent ensured that Canada participated in the war on the side of the South. St. Laurent also helped bring a peaceful resolution to the Suez Crisis in 1956 by supporting the establishment of the first peacekeeping force in the world.

Milestones:

- Invested in welfare programs like old age pensions and building programs for roads, schools, power plants, and other important projects
- Supported the building of the Trans-Canada Highway and the St. Lawrence Seaway

The Suez Crisis

The Suez Canal is an important route for ships moving oil from the Middle East to Europe. In 1956, Egypt seized control of the shipping route. It also prevented ships from Israel access to the canal. Britain, France, and Israel invaded Egypt to try to regain control of the Canal, against the wishes of the US, Canada, and other countries.

Lester Pearson, a Canadian diplomat working under Louis St. Laurent, came up with a solution to the "Suez Crisis." He proposed the creation of the first United Nations peacekeeping force. This force supervised the withdrawal of British, French, and Israeli troops from Egypt and the reopening of the canal, stopping a potential war.

Canadian soldiers fly out to join UN peacekeeping forces to help police the Suez situation.

John Diefenbaker
Champion of the Underdog

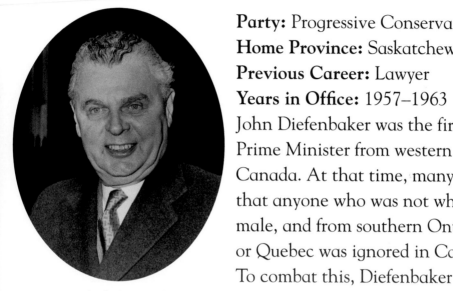

Party: Progressive Conservative
Home Province: Saskatchewan
Previous Career: Lawyer
Years in Office: 1957–1963
John Diefenbaker was the first
Prime Minister from western
Canada. At that time, many felt
that anyone who was not white,
male, and from southern Ontario
or Quebec was ignored in Canada.
To combat this, Diefenbaker
extended the right to vote to include all First Nations people
in Canada. He also appointed the first woman to the Cabinet
and the first person of First Nations origin to the Senate.

Diefenbaker's time in office was complicated by a
controversy over an agreement he made with the US. The
agreement allowed the US to locate missiles equipped with
nuclear weapons on Canadian soil. Later on, Diefenbaker
tried to back out of the agreement. The flip flop led to the
eventual fall of his government.

The Avro Arrow was an advanced supersonic fighter jet
developed in Canada. When Canada decided to host American
missiles, the project was scrapped. It cost Canada millions of
dollars of investment and thousands of Canadian jobs.

Milestones:

- Extended voting rights to Indigenous peoples
- Removed racial discrimination from immigration policy
- Introduced the Bill of Rights, which eventually became the current Charter of Rights and Freedoms

The "Diefenbunker" is one of the most visited tourist sites near Ottawa. It is a massive underground bunker that was designed during Diefenbaker's time in office to keep the Canadian government safe from a nuclear attack. This once top-secret bunker was designed to house over 500 people for more than a month!

The blast tunnel in the Diefenbunker was designed to direct the force of an explosion away from the main part of the bunker.

Lester B. Pearson
The Peacekeeper

Party: Liberal
Home Province: Ontario
Previous Career: Diplomat
Years in Office: 1963–1968
Before becoming PM, Lester Pearson came up with the idea of the UN peacekeeping force that solved the Suez Crisis (see p.75). His work in peacekeeping earned him a Nobel Peace Prize in 1957.

Pearson was very involved in the governments of King and St. Laurent, and once he was elected PM he mostly continued their policies of social reform. Many social programs that Canadians take for granted today were introduced or expanded during Pearson's time in office. These include universal health care and the Canada Pension Plan (a program to provide money to people after they stop working at the age of 65).

Pearson started a study on bilingualism. He also ensured that Canada did not participate in the Vietnam War. This did not make him popular with US President Lyndon Johnson, who wanted Canada to support America's efforts in the war.

At the end of Pearson's term in office, the French President Charles de Gaulle visited Quebec and gave a speech of huge importance in Canadian history. The speech ended with the historic phrase "vive le Québec libre"—long live a free Quebec.

The speech ignited the spark of Quebec nationalism. A movement called Separatism became popular, in which Quebeckers grew determined to separate from Canada and form a new independent country. The separatist threat would cause problems for Prime Ministers for years to come.

Milestones:

- Merged the Canadian Army, the Royal Canadian Airforce, and the Royal Canadian Navy into the Canadian Forces
- Oversaw the creation of the new Canadian flag
- Created the Canada Pension Plan

Canada's flag was created during Pearson's time in office. Before that, Canada did not have an official flag. The flags commonly flown were designs based on the British flag and Canadian symbols. Pearson wanted a flag that would be unique and unmistakably Canadian.

Coming up with a new design started what came to be known as "The Great Flag Debate." More than 2000 designs, many contributed by the general public, were

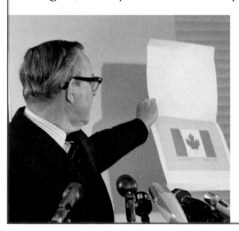

considered. Finally, the current red-and-white design featuring the Maple Leaf was chosen by a unanimous vote by a Parliamentary committee.

Pearson shows off the design for Canada's new flag at a press conference in 1964.

Pierre Elliot Trudeau
The Pirouetting PM

Party: Liberal
Home Province: Quebec
Previous Career: Lawyer and Professor
Years in Office: 1968–1979
1980–1984

Pierre Trudeau was unlike any other Prime Minister in Canadian history. His big personality caught the attention of the media and Canadians, inspiring "Trudeaumania" (see p.61). In the early years of his time in office, he was probably the most popular Prime Minister in Canadian history.

Trudeau soon passed many important reforms. These included making English and French the official languages of Canada. In 1982, he succeeded in patriating the Canadian Constitution—freeing Canada from being controlled by Great Britain's Parliament (see p.14).

Trudeau fought fiercely against Quebec separatism (see p.78–79). In 1970, a terrorist organization

Pierre Trudeau carries his son Justin into Rideau Hall in 1973. Justin Trudeau later became Prime Minister himself in 2015.

that supported Quebec independence called the FLQ (Front Liberation du Québec) kidnapped and murdered a provincial politician. Trudeau took decisive action. He called in the Canadian military, using the War Measures Act—the only time this has been done during a time of peace in Canadian history. The tense situation, which came to be known as the October Crisis, finally ended when members of the FLQ flew to exile in Cuba. Others were arrested and sent to prison for murder. Later, in 1980, Quebec held their first referendum to decide if they would separate from Canada. Trudeau campaigned strongly against the "Yes"-voting separatists, and the "No" votes won, 59.5 percent to 40.5 percent.

Milestones:

- Repatriated the Canadian Constitution
- Created the Charter of Rights and Freedoms (see p.14)
- Created a policy of national bilingualism and multiculturalism

Trudeau was known for his sharp wit and self-confidence. When a reporter asked him how far he would go to solve the October Crisis, Trudeau famously responded by saying "just watch me."

Using the War Measures Act was an unpopular decision with some people because the Act suspended the personal rights and freedoms of Canadians.

Brian Mulroney
The Confident Capitalist

Party: Progressive Conservative
Home Province: Quebec
Previous Career: Lawyer
Years in Office: 1984–1993
When Brian Mulroney was first elected, his party had one of the largest majorities in history. He left office, however, when his party suffered the worst election performance in Canadian history. The Progressive Conservatives won only two seats in the House of Commons!

During his time in office Mulroney focused mainly on the economy and constitutional reform. He was close friends with US president Ronald Reagan. Together, they negotiated and signed a historic trade agreement with Mexico called the North American Free Trade Agreement (NAFTA). This Agreement helped to lower or get rid of fees that were charged when goods were moved (imported or exported) between the three countries. He also introduced some environmental protections, including a treaty with the US that greatly reduced air pollution and the damage caused by acid rain in southwestern Ontario.

On the international stage Mulroney was one of the fiercest opponents of the Apartheid government in South Africa.

Apartheid was a racist system of government in South Africa from 1948 to 1994. It separated people by race, so where you lived, worked, went to school, shopped, and more depended on the colour of your skin. White people were given better services and more rights than other people.

So why had Mulroney, and his party, grown so unpopular? The later years of Mulroney's government were taken up by trying to make changes to the Constitution (see p.55–57). The changes failed, leaving him as one of the least popular Prime Ministers when he left office.

Milestones:
- Signed a free trade agreement with the United States nd Mexico
- Strongly opposed the Apartheid government in South Africa
- Took steps to protect the environment
- Introduced the very unpopular Goods and Services Tax (GST)

Kim Campbell won the Progressive Conservative Party leadership race and took over as PM when Brian Mulroney retired from office. She was the first woman to serve as Canada's Prime Minister. She was Prime Minister for less than five months before she was defeated in an election. Her once record-high support plummeted after Canadians thought her party mocked Jean Chrétien's appearance in a campaign ad (see p.35).

Jean Chrétien
The Anti-Separatist

Party: Liberal
Home Province: Quebec
Previous Career: Lawyer
Years in Office: 1993–2003

Jean Chrétien's time in office was dominated by the issue of Quebec separatism, which had attracted a large number of followers in Quebec, along with relations with the US, and the notorious "Sponsorship Scandal" (see p.64).

Ever since French president Charles de Gaulle visited Quebec in 1967 (see p.78), many people in Quebec had wanted Quebec to be independent of Canada. Chrétien was a Quebec native but a strong federalist—a believer in a united Canada.

Everything came to a head in 1995 when Quebec held a second referendum to decide if they would like to separate from Canada. If the majority of the population of Quebec voted to separate, they would ask the federal government for the right to remove themselves from the Confederation.

The entire country was in an uproar. Many feared what would happen if the province voted to separate. They foresaw economic ruin, and years of constitutional negotiation that would take away from Canada's growth

Jean Chrétien campaigns for a unified Canada.

Supporters of the Quebec separatist movement march to support the "yes" side.

and prosperity. Others thought Quebec should be free to go if they no longer wished to be part of the Canadian nation.

On the night of October 30, 1995, the separatists were defeated by a very narrow margin, barely one percent. Canada's ten provinces would remain together, for now.

During his term in office, Chrétien also worked with the US to try to end several international crises. Canada sent troops to the war in Kosovo in 1999 and participated in the invasion of Afghanistan in 2002 after the 9/11 attacks on New York City's World Trade Towers.

The end of Chrétien's time in office was consumed by the Sponsorship Scandal, forcing him to retire.

Milestones:

- Helped to defeat Quebec Separatism in the 1995 referendum
- Eliminated the budget deficit, meaning that the government was not spending more than it earned
- Created the Harmonized Sales Tax (HST), which combined a federal and provincial sales tax in some provinces

Stephen Harper
The Chief Conservative

Party: Conservative
Home Province: Ontario
Previous Career: Politician
Years in Office: 2006–2015

Stephen Harper spent much of his time in office trying to direct the recovery of the Canadian economy and dealing with the ongoing war in Afghanistan. In 2008, an economic crisis in the US spread to Canada, just as it had during the Great Depression. It caused massive unemployment and social unrest.

Harper's government reduced taxes, provided money for job training and to support struggling businesses, and put more money into building roads, schools, tourism, and other big projects to help keep jobs for Canadians.

Harper poses with medal winners from the 2010 Winter Olympics. The games stimulated a wave of Canadian pride and patriotism across the country.

Harper's government provided strong support for Canadian athletes, leading to Canada's best performance ever at the Olympic games in the 2010 Winter Olympics held in Vancouver.

Protestors demonstrate against Harper's decision to prorogue Parliament.

During his term in office, Harper was strongly criticized for abusing the rules of Parliament. He asked the Governor General to *prorogue*, or temporarily stop, parliament four times, once to avoid a no-confidence vote. This was seen as unfair and against the principles of democracy. Harper was also criticized for seeming to place the interests of industry over the environment.

Milestones:

- Oversaw new projects to help stimulate the economy
- Prorogued parliament
- Apologized for the mistreatment of Indigenous Canadians under the Residential School System

In 2008, Harper officially apologized to Canada's Indigenous people for the mistreatment and abuse of the residential school system, a longstanding, nation-wide system that removed the children of Indigenous people from their homes and placed them in a government-run school. The system was meant to help to integrate the children into western society, but it only served to isolate them from their own culture and identity.

Justin Trudeau
The "Sunny Way" PM

Party: Liberal
Home Province: Ontario
Previous Career: Teacher
Years in Office: 2015–

Justin Trudeau, son of Pierre Trudeau, is the only child of a former Prime Minister to have been elected Prime Minister. He was elected into office in the fall of 2015. In his acceptance speech, he quoted Sir Wilfred Laurier's expression of choosing the "sunny way," meaning that his government was intending to be fair and respectful of different viewpoints. Thanks to his youth, charm, and good looks, he became a favourite with the media and was able to capture some of the "Trudeaumania" that his father had inspired almost 50 years earlier.

Prime Minister Justin Trudeau greets veterans at the Remembrance Day ceremony in Ottawa in 2016.

Trudeau made a point of making his government inclusive of all Canadians.

Milestones:

- Created a Cabinet with an even split between women and men, a first in Canadian history
- Committed to championing the rights of the First Nations
- Signed the Paris climate treaty to help fight climate change
- Accepted more than 25,000 refugees from the Syrian civil war into Canada

Now it's your turn!

Canada's government is both simple and complex. Simple, because it allows for the people to rule themselves. And complex, because it involves many people and strict rules and procedures to make that happen. Its great strength is that it allows for all kinds of people, from all backgrounds, to live together in harmony.

Canada's government works best when more people—people like you—participate. You can take an active role in Canada's government by joining the youth wing of a political party. You can express your opinion to your MP easily by mailing a letter (postage to an MP is free!) or sending an email. You can also attend sittings in the House of Commons and the Senate, or watch them online or on TV. When you are old enough, you can vote in elections. Perhaps one day you will even decide to run for office! If so, you can help create the laws that will shape Canada's—and your—future.

Our Great Prime Ministers Quiz

See if you can remember the answers to these questions about what you have read.

1. What are the three main political parties in Canada?

2. In what year did Canada gain full independence from Great Britain?

3. Who was the longest serving Prime Minister?

4. Which branch of the government is the Prime Minister the head of?

5. Who represents the Monarch (Queen/King) in Canada?

6. Which Prime Minister won a Nobel Peace Prize in 1957?

7. Which type of government is in charge of public transit?

8. What is Canada's official motto?

9. Which is the largest election riding in Canada, geographically?

10. Senators may serve in the Senate until what age?

11. Which Prime Minister had an underground bunker built in case of a nuclear war?

12. Which Prime Minister is the son of a former Prime Minister?

13. What kind of government is formed when a party wins the majority of seats in the House of Commons, but less than half?

14. How long can a Prime Minister stay in office without being re-elected?

15. How old does a Canadian citizen have to be to be able to vote in a federal election?

Glossary

Advocate
To support and promote a person, an idea, or an interest.

Appeal
To ask a higher court to reverse the decision of a lower court.

Appoint
To give a position to someone, instead of selecting them through an *election*.

Ballot
A piece of paper used to cast a vote.

Bill
A proposed *law*.

By-law
Any *law* made by a city (municipal) government instead of the federal or provincial governments. For example, a city can make a by-law that gives rules for parking cars. The rules will apply only in that city.

Cabinet
Advisors to the Prime Minister.

Coalition
Two or more political parties that have joined together, usually temporarily, to have more power.

Constituents
People who live in a particular election *riding*.

Constitution
A set of rules that tells how a government will be run.

Constitutional monarchy
A country that has a monarch (king/ queen), but the monarch's powers are limited by a constitution.

Debate
An organized, often public, discussion between two or more people with different views.

Democracy
A government where citizens choose the people who will govern (be in charge of the country) by voting.

Diplomat
A person who represents their own country's government abroad.

Diversity
A range of different races, cultures, sexes, and religions in a population.

Election
To select someone by voting for them.

Executive branch
The part of the government that makes sure *laws* and decisions are carried out. It is made up of the Prime Minister and the *Cabinet*.

Federal
Country-wide or national.

Indigenous people
People who lived in Canada before the arrival of European settlers. These include First Nations, the Métis, and the Inuit.

Interpret
To explain the meaning of.

Judicial branch
The part of the government that interprets and applies *laws*.

Law
A rule that says what is and what is not allowed.

Leadership convention
A gathering of a political party to vote for a new leader for the party.

Legislative branch
The part of the government that makes new *laws* or changes old ones.

Member of Parliament (MP)
A person elected to the House of Commons to represent a region of Canada.

Minority groups
A group of people that are different in some way (for example, religion, race, or language) to most of the population.

Monarch
A king or queen.

No Confidence
A vote that shows that the Members of Parliament do not believe the government and the Prime Minister are doing their job well. If it is passed, a vote of No Confidence will trigger an *election*.

Parliamentary Democracy
A type of government where the citizens elect representatives to a parliament to make *laws* and decisions for the country.

Party platform
The views and promises of a political party made during an election campaign.

Policy
A set of plans or ideas on what to do in a particular situation, made by a government or a political party.

Premier
The leader of a provincial or territorial government.

Prorogue
To temporarily stop a session of parliament without dissolving the government.

Referendum
A public vote on a particular issue.

Riding
A voting region.

Taxes
Money collected by a government from its citizens to pay for facilities and services such as health care.

Treaty
An agreement between two or more countries.

Unbiased
To show no preference for one thing over another; to be fair.

93

Guide for Parents

DK Readers is a four-level interactive reading adventure series for children, developing the habit of reading widely for both pleasure and information. These books have an exciting main narrative interspersed with a range of reading genres to suit your child's reading ability. Each book is designed to develop your child's reading skills, fluency, grammar awareness, and comprehension in order to build confidence and engagement when reading.

Ready for a *Reading Alone* book

YOUR CHILD SHOULD

- be able to read independently and silently for extended periods of time.
- read aloud flexibly and fluently, in expressive phrases with the listener in mind.
- be able to respond to what is being read and be able to discuss key ideas in the text.

A VALUABLE AND SHARED READING EXPERIENCE

Supporting children when they are reading proficiently can encourage them to value reading and to view reading as an interesting, purposeful, and enjoyable pastime. So here are a few tips on how to use this book with your child.

TIP 1 Reading aloud as a learning opportunity:

- after your child has read a part of the book, ask him/her to tell you what has happened so far.
- even though your child may be reading independently, most children at this level still enjoy having a parent read aloud.
- Take turns reading sections of the book, especially sections that contain dialogue that can provide practice in expressive reading.

TIP 2 Chat at the end of each chapter:

- encourage your child to recall specific details after each chapter.
- let your child pick out interesting words and discuss what they mean.
- talk about what each of you found most interesting or most important.
- ask the questions provided in the quiz at the back of the book. These help to develop comprehension skills and awareness of the language used.
- ask if there's anything that your child would like to discover more about.

Further information can be researched in the index of other nonfiction books or on the Internet.

A FEW ADDITIONAL TIPS

- Continue to read to your child regularly to demonstrate fluency, phrasing and expression; to find out or check information; and for sharing enjoyment.
- Encourage your child to read a range of different genres, such as newspapers, poems, review articles and instructions.
- Provide opportunities for your child to read to a variety of eager listeners, such as a sibling or a grandparent.

Helaine Becker is an award-winning writer of children's books, both fiction and nonfiction, including *A Porcupine in a Pine Tree*, *Worms for Breakfast*, and *Monster Science*. She also writes for children's magazines and television and is a popular presenter and performer at schools across Canada.

Michael Szasz teaches English to grade two students in Guangzhou, China, where he often dreams of poutine and butter tarts. He is the co-author of National Geographic Kids *Everything: Space* and enjoys travel, history, and e-sports.

Index

apartheid 82, 83

Avro Arrow 76

Bennett, Richard B. 58, 62–63, 65

Bill of Rights 77

Borden, Sir Robert 58, 65, 70–71

British Commonwealth 13

British North America Act 12, 14

Cabinet 19, 20, 41–42, 45

campaign, election 33–36

Campbell, Kim 65, 83

Canada Pension Plan 78, 79

Canadian Forces 79

Canadian Pacific Railway 66, 67

Charlottetown Accord 57

Charter of Rights and Freedoms 14, 15, 53–54, 77, 81

   Notwithstanding Clause 54

Chief Electoral Officer 29

Chinese head tax 67

Chrétien, Jean 27, 35, 65, 84–85

Clark, Joe 35–36, 65

colonies 8–9

   British 9, 10–13

   French 9

Confederation, Canadian 10–14

conscription 70–71, 72

Constitution, Canadian 14–15, 28, 53–57

   changes to 14–15, 55–57

   Constitution Act 14, 15

   repatriation of 14–15, 55, 80

constitutional monarchy 8

de Gaulle, Charles 78, 84

democracy 6–7

Diefenbaker, John 60, 65, 76–77

Diefenbunker 77

Dominion of Canada 12

election, federal 28–37

   Elections Canada 35, 37

   voting in 29, 36–37

Executive Branch 19, 20, 21, 24

flag, Canadian 79

   Great Flag Debate 79

Front Liberation du Québec (FLQ) 81

G-20 summit 60

government

   branches of 19–23

   coalition 39

   federal 12, 16–17, 19–23

   majority 38–39

   minority 38–39

   municipal 17–18

   provincial 17

Governor General 15, 20, 23, 48, 51

Great Depression 62–63, 72, 86

Harper, Stephen 37, 48, 60, 65, 67, 86–87

House of Commons 19, 20, 21–22

immigration policy 67, 77

Indigenous people 30, 57, 76, 77, 87

Japanese-Canadian internment camps 73

John, King of England 7, 8

Judicial Branch 19, 20, 22–23

   Federal Court 20, 23

   Provincial Court 20, 23

   Supreme Court 20, 22

King, William Lyon Mackenzie 28, 62–63, 72–73

Laurier, Sir Wilfrid 58, 65, 68–69

laws 48–51

leadership convention 27

League of Nations 71

Legislative Branch 19, 20, 21, 22

Macdonald, Sir John A. 11, 34, 47, 55, 65, 66–67

Mackenzie, Alexander 11, 58, 65, 69

Magna Carta 7, 8

Martin, Paul 27, 34, 64, 65

Meech Lake Accord 56, 57

Member of Parliament 21, 22, 30, 38, 42–43, 45–47

monarch 7, 8, 13, 14, 15, 20, 23

Mulroney, Brian 32, 55–57, 65, 82–83

No Confidence vote 29, 87

North American Free Trade Agreement (NAFTA) 82

North Atlantic Treaty Organization (NATO) 74

October Crisis 81

opposition parties 26, 27, 39, 41

   official 5, 26, 27, 45

Paris climate treaty 89

parliamentary democracy 6, 7

parties, political 24–25

   Bloc Québécois 25, 26

   Conservative Party 24, 25

   Green Party 25, 26

   Liberal Party 24, 26

   New Democratic Party 25, 26

   Rhinoceros Party 25

Pearson, Lester B. 65, 75, 78–79

police 18, 52

polling station 36, 37

Premiers 17, 48

Prime Ministers 58–89

   complete list of 65

   French Canadian 58, 68, 74,

   roles, responsibilities, and duties 59–64

prorogue 87

Provinces, joining Confederation 13

Question Period 45–46

Reagan, Ronald 82

referendum 57, 81, 84, 85

Residential School System 87

riding 30–32

Riel, Louis 67

Royal Assent 51

scandals 63–64

   Sponsorship Scandal 64, 84, 85

Senate 19, 20, 21–22, 43–45, 50–51

   senator 21, 22, 43–44

Separatism 79, 80–81, 84–85

September 11 attacks 85

Shadow Cabinet 41

St. Laurent, Louis 65, 74–75

St. Lawrence Seaway 75

Suez Crisis 74, 75, 78

Taxes 52–53

   Goods and Services Tax (GST) 83

   Harmonized Sales Tax (HST) 52, 85

Trans-Canada Highway 75

Trudeau, Justin 4, 21, 26, 42, 47, 65, 88–89

Trudeau, Pierre Elliot 14, 36, 55, 65, 80–81

   Trudeaumania 61

Tupper, Charles 28, 65

UN peacekeeping force 74–75, 78

voting 29, 36–37

   right to vote 29, 30, 54, 71, 76

wars

   Afghanistan War 85, 86

   Boer War 68

   Korean War 74

   Kosovo 1999 85

   Seven Years' War 9

   Syrian civil war 89

   Vietnam War 78

   War Measures Act 81

   World War I 70, 71

   Treaty of Versailles 71

   World War II 72, 73